Freedom Crossing

By Quito Keutla

Copyright © 2017 Quito Keutla

All rights reserved. Except for use in any review, no part of this publication may be reproduced, distributed, or transmitted in any form or by any means now known or hereafter invented, or stored in a database or retrieval system, without the prior written permission of the author.

This book is dedicated to our parents who made the courageous decision to cross the great Mekong River for a better future for their children. Our love for you, Mom and Dad, goes beyond words, and the example you set for us has made us who we are today.

From the mid to late 1900s, Laos saw a lot of government instability, going from being a French protectorate to Japanese occupation, the return of French rule, and eventually a constitutional monarchy in 1953. The independence was short-lived, however, when a long civil war ended the monarchy, and in 1975, communist rule settled on this small landlocked country, where it still exists today.

Over the next 25 years, more than three million people would risk their lives for freedom—for a chance at a life without fear.

Hard Decision

As my siblings and I prepare to gather for my parents' wedding anniversary, we can't help but count our blessings. We have family, freedom, and security. In short, the American Dream.

And it's all thanks to our parents, who risked everything to give their children a chance at that dream. A chance to live without the fear and oppression that came with the communist rule that settled over our home country of Laos. It may have been almost 40 years since our family made its daring escape across the Mekong River, but it's a story we shall never forget.

When the Pathet Lao established communist rule over Laos in 1975, my family and I were living in the capitol city of Vientiane, Laos. My father, Sisavath, worked as a surveyor for the government, which had him spending most of his time in Vietnam. This left my mother, Khanthaly, who also worked for the government as a secretary, to raise the five of us on her own. While being a state employee usually meant security and stability in other countries, this was not the case for Laotians. The paychecks were barely enough to support us, if they were handed out at all. In an effort to make sure we had enough to eat, my father would teach surveying in what little spare time he had.

For this reason, my youngest sister, Khuanmany, was being raised by my father's oldest brother and his wife, who had been unable to have any children of their own despite years of trying. Even I was often sent to stay with other members of my father's family for extended periods of time.

Over time, the distance between my mother and father, along with the stress of trying to provide for us children, became more and more unbearable for Mom. Meanwhile, my mother would hear stories of other Laotians fleeing the country for the chance at a better and safer future. She would see pictures of people who had made the journey to other lands, but attempting our own escape didn't cross her mind.

Then in 1980, my mother hit a breaking point after my father had been gone for an entire year. Even though she was kept busy with work and caring for my siblings and me, the heartache was too much. Throughout her day she would see other families out and about—husbands and wives raising their children together. They looked so happy to have each other. And it was a painful reminder of what she and my father were missing out on.

"I don't know how much more of this I can take," she confided to a friend one day as they made their way into work.

"You should leave," her friend said.

"Leave?" Mom scoffed. "Where would I go to? What would that do?"

"Leave Laos," the friend said quietly. "You should escape. As others have done."

"But isn't that dangerous? And *illegal*?"

Her friend shrugged, and my mother was ready to brush it off, but she found her thoughts drifting back to the idea over and over.

Father finally came home for a meeting, and my mother was so relieved to have her husband home again, even if she knew it would only be for a short time.

For the first time, that evening we enjoyed a family supper together, everyone laughing at the funny stories my father liked to tell us.

"I have to leave again in the morning," he told my mother as they crawled into bed later that night.

But she wasn't ready to say goodbye again so soon.

"I've been thinking," she told him in the dark. "What if we were to leave Laos? We could start a new life somewhere else. A better life."

"No," he immediately responded.

"Why not?" she asked, hurt that he was dismissing the idea so quickly.

"Because we have jobs to do. We have a family to think about."

"I *am* thinking about our family. Don't you want more for them?"

"It's too dangerous, though," he said.

"If you don't want to come," she said, turning her back to him, "then maybe the next time you come home, we won't be here."

"Khanthaly," he sighed, rolling over to put an arm around her. "You can't actually mean that."

"I suppose you'll just have to find out, won't you," she said, unsure that she would actually have the courage to do it without him.

There was no more talk of escaping that night, and while she was disappointed at his refusal to entertain the idea, my mother held her husband a little tighter, wishing he didn't have to go away in the morning. Or ever again.

The next morning my father got up and ready for work.

"I have to go," he said to my mother. "I have to do my job."

She nodded, and he was relieved when she still decided to ride along with him to the airport, to give him a chance to spend even a few more minutes with her. Who knew how long it would be until he could embrace his wife again?

When they arrived, my mother sat in the taxi, waiting to watch his helicopter take off and wondering if there would ever come a day when they didn't have to be apart so much.

"This stupid job of his," she muttered to herself in frustration.

Then, to her surprise, my father was walking back to the taxi.

"Is everything okay?" she asked as he climbed in next to her.

"Apparently the helicopter isn't working," he said. "They told me to come back in a few days. It should be fixed by then."

"You know," my mother said while they made their way back home. "This would be a good time to escape." She watched his brow crease. "What do you think?"

He sat there next to her, quiet for the longest time.

"Maybe…" he finally answered, turning to her. "Would you know how we could do it?"

"I have a friend," she said, her heart racing. "She knows what to do, who to hire. Just say the word and she can help us.

"No one is expecting me for the next couple days."

My mother nodded excitedly.

"Okay," he said. "Let's do it."

My mother was immediately optimistic, thinking only of the future that was waiting for them. But even though he had agreed to try, he was already worrying, imagining the dangers they would have to face before they even made it to the refugee camp in Thailand. While Mom was remembering the people who had made it, the pictures she had seen of the successful refugees, he was remembering the stories of people who hadn't made it. He knew that anyone who was caught trying to escape Laos would be killed. It was a fear so great, he'd heard of people successfully crossing the Mekong River only to turn back.

And the ones who hadn't crossed successfully…their bodies would be left to drift down the river, and then pillaged by the struggling farmers who found them.

Going for a Visit

Before they could leave, Mom and Dad needed to get Khuanmany. So after swinging by home to let Auntie know they would be back in a few days, they had the cab drop them off at a bus station.

After a day's ride, they arrived at Uncle's house and as my mother stood there, holding Khuanmany in her arms while Dad spoke with his older brother, their two-year-old daughter started to fuss in her arms.

"Shh," Mother hushed, gently bouncing her on a hip. "Don't cry, don't cry." But Khuanmany wouldn't quiet down. Mother looked up at Father in a panic; she could see her own fears on his face. How could they ever escape with a crying toddler?

"Sie, what do we do?" she asked.

"We'll have to leave her," he said reluctantly.

"But she's my baby," Mother said, fighting back tears. "I can't leave her."

"If we bring her, she could get us all killed."

She looked down at Khuanmany and kissed her forehead, knowing it was true.

"We'll come back for her. After we get settled somewhere else and can afford it. We'll come back."

"Of course," my father told her, hugging his wife and youngest child, and thought to himself, if they didn't make it through, at least one of his children would still be alive.

And so rather than leaving Uncle's with Khuanmany, they were forced to say their goodbyes to her, hoping it wouldn't be the last time they saw her.

We were playing in the area behind our house with my siblings when our parents returned.

FREEDOM CROSSING

"Kids," mother called, getting our attention. "We're going to visit my best friend for a couple days. Go get ready."

All of us looked at each other with eyes wide. Most of us had never gone out of town before. It sounded so exciting.

"Yes, Mom," Lucky, the oldest, said. Tobee, Leh, and I followed her inside to grab a few items to take with us—not that we had much to pack.

Mom pulled out her sewing supplies and unhooked her gold bracelet, the most valuable thing she owned. Knowing she would need to pay whoever was going to help us, she pulled off what she estimated to be about one ounce worth of gold, a third of the links, from the bracelet. She then sewed the rest of it into the waistband of her sarong. As she tied it back around her waist, Mom felt confident that this would prevent the only currency they had from being lost or stolen.

Being only six and with Khuanmany having spent most of her two years with Uncle, I didn't even realize that I wasn't the youngest. So as we headed to the nearby Talat Sao (local market) where we could catch a taxi, it didn't even occur to me that a member of our family was being left behind.

Lucky, who was nine at the time, had a better recollection of our youngest sister. Yet seeing as how we were just going to visit Mom's best friend, she didn't find it any more unusual than I did.

My parents, Tobee, and I piled onto our motorcycle, an unsafe practice that is still just as common in Laos today as it was then. Lucky and Leh rode with Auntie on her bicycle. Lucky noticed the mix of emotions on our Auntie's face as they made their way to the market. Auntie, who was carrying Lucky and Leh on her bicycle, looked both happy and distraught to my oldest sister.

"What's wrong?" Lucky asked her.

"Wrong? Nothing's wrong," Auntie told her. "I'm excited for you."

Even though Auntie was smiling, Lucky could see the sadness in her eyes as well.

When they got to market, she caught Auntie talking with our mother. Even though Lucky couldn't hear what they were saying, she could tell by the look on her face that Auntie was worried, crying even. What was there to be so upset about, Lucky wondered. They were only going to visit Mom's best friend. They would all be home again soon. Yet Lucky couldn't help feeling sad for one of her favorite aunties.

To our surprise, Dad announced that we could have any soda we wanted—a rare treat.

Lucky ordered Sunkist, and to this day, she'll still tell you it's her favorite drink.

While we sipped our soda, excited to have it, Mom and Dad didn't seem nearly as cheerful, as they kept looking over their shoulders.

Eventually someone approached my parents, who were immediately apprehensive.

"Are you Khanthaly?" the man asked.

"I am," my mother replied, knowing this must be the smuggler who had been hired to get them out of the city.

"Come with me."

Our parents announced it was time to go, so we bid our auntie goodbye and followed them to a taxi. The Stranger climbed into the driver's seat, and we piled in the back with Dad in the front next to the stranger.

It was crowded in the back, with our bodies bumping against each other every time the cab went over a rock or pot hole on the unmaintained dirt road. I remember it was hot in that car and not very pleasant. I'm not sure how long the ride was, but we were all anticipating when we would get to our destination so we could jump out and breathe some fresh air.

Finally the cab came to a stop when we reached a house in the remote countryside. To our disappointment, we were told to remain in the cab as our parents got out.

"Stay here," my mother said. She and Dad walked up to the house. There were several homes in that area, all built on 8-foot poles to protect them during the monsoon seasons, as was common out in the countryside.

Someone came out of the house as my parents approached the stairs leading up to the small covered porch.

"Are you Khanthaly?" they asked, and she nodded. "Inside now. Quietly."

Dad turned to the taxi, waving for us to join them. Finally we all climbed out and made our way up to the front door as the taxi drove off.

We assumed this must be our mom's friend's house. Inside was just one large room with an opening, like a window, but without any glass.

"If you go by there," my father said, practically whispering, "make sure you duck. Make sure no one sees you. Okay?"

All of us kids nodded. We didn't understand why, or even who would see us, as no one seemed to be around at this time of day. But being the obedient children that we were, we did as they asked.

"Go play," Mom told us, "just remember to be quiet."

Again, we nodded.

As Dad watched us play, making sure we didn't do anything to expose us, he found himself on edge, listening for any noise that might mean trouble. Then he heard it. The crunch of tires coming down the dirt road. Had they been found so soon? Had someone followed them from Vientiane?

His heart raced as he heard a vehicle stop outside the house, and then a door slamming closed. Footsteps came up the steps. Father looked around quickly, assessing an exit or a weapon. Could they lie their way out of this?

There was a knock at the door. The homeowner, the same man who had met us, went over to it cautiously. Dad waited with bated breath as the door opened, and he saw a man's face, uncertain and anxious, on the other side.

"Vannaseng?" the owner of the house asked, and the new person nodded. "Inside, quickly."

The man disappeared and returned again with his wife and two children.

My father tried to calm his nerves and looked at his children playing quietly, reminding himself why they were doing this.

That night a dinner was prepared—some kind of pork chop and a papaya salad. We sat there quietly eating. The excitement of the day had worn all of us kids out, but my parents were lost in thought.

My mother was surely envisioning how close we were to freedom, to a new life, while my father's thought were less optimistic.

As he looked around at his family, eating this meal together, it occurred to him that this might very well be our last meal together, and he fought back the emotions that swept over him.

After dinner, our family gathered in the middle part of the house and went to sleep—except for my father, who was still second-guessing the decision he had made that very morning. What if they were caught? What if someone had noticed them leaving Vientiane and arriving at the house? What if the boat flipped while they crossed the river? None of his children could swim. Even if he was able to save them from drowning, would the armed guards find them before they found safety?

As he listened to the tossing and turning of his children, the soft breaths of his wife sleeping on his chest, he finally let the tears fall, knowing that in the next few hours, they would all either be dead…or free from the Laotian government.

Crossing the River

In the middle of the night, there was a knock at the door—someone telling us it was time to go. My parents quickly woke us up.

We were confused. Were we already going back home? Why were we doing this in the middle of the night? We were being told to take off our shoes and carry them as we rushed out the door. Leh, who was just getting over a cold, coughed as we got outside.

"Cover your mouth," my dad said quickly. "Try not to cough."

FREEDOM CROSSING

Feeling a little afraid, Leh realized we must be doing something we're not supposed to, but she did as Dad said. We were all together, so how bad could it be?

Mom took Lucky and Leh's hand while Dad had me and Tobee. We were led through the sugar cane fields by two men—the smugglers who had been hired to get us to Thailand. The two men didn't carry flashlights or candles with us and were relying on the moonlight to guide us on the path.

The ground was hard beneath our bare feet, and we wondered how far we had to go, but nobody made any noise, only Leh's cough every now and then, followed by a panicked look from the grownups.

We were nearing the jungle at the edge of the field when one of the two smugglers pulled out a giant knife, and my mother's heart stopped as she caught the glint of moonlight on the blade. She pulled Lucky and Leh tight against her, sure that the whole thing had been a scam and now they were about to be robbed and killed. But then he simply hacked down one of the stalks and started chewing on the pulp, sucking out the fresh sugar cane juice. Relieved, my mother let out a quiet sigh. She was afraid, as she had heard that some of these men hired to "help" them may have only been in it for the money and cared very little about the people they were helping.

The group kept marching along.

With sore feet we reached the shore of the Mekong River. The two men disappeared into some nearby bushes. The river was calm as it flowed along the Laos border, but it was an illusion. Being over a mile wide, the Mekong was a deep river that ran with a mighty and powerful current.

I remember the smell of fish and decay coming off of it just as the men reappeared from the bushes dragging an old wooden fishing canoe.

"Get in," one of the men told us. "Everybody, get in. Hurry!"

My parents looked at the group of us, our two families plus the two men telling us what to do, and then to the tiny boat. They couldn't all be expected to fit in a boat designed for only four fishermen.

"Isn't there another boat?" my mom asked.

"No," he told her. "If you want to cross the river, you'll get in this boat."

We all climbed in, squeezing wherever we could, half the kids sitting on the other half's laps.

By the time we pushed off from the shore, the water surface was barely an inch from the lip of the boat.

FREEDOM CROSSING

As we made our way across the river, the only sound we heard was the oars slipping in and out of the water, punctuated every now and then by Leh stifling her cough. We were losing sight of the shore we had just been standing on, sailing away into nothing. Was there another shore? Would we ever reach it?

Suddenly a crack cut through the silence, and everyone looked around for its source, muttering in fear.

"Quiet," one of the smugglers said in a rough whisper. "It's just the oar." Everyone looked to see him holding half a paddle, the bottom of it jagged where it had snapped off, just before he let it slide into the river. The paddle wasn't strong enough paddling so many people. We all quieted down and he cocked an ear, listening for any indication that someone else had heard the sound.

With only one oar and the river's current being so strong, the boat slowly spun, its bow turning down river. That meant we were no longer headed toward the Thai shore. Dad and the other father quickly slipped a sandal onto their hands and paddled as fast and hard as they could. The smuggler did the same, and soon the boat was back on course.

As my father dragged his arm through the dark water, in and out, he glimpsed the trunk of a banana tree floating down the river. Holding his breath, he scanned it for signs of a body. He'd heard stories of the Hmong, most of whom were unable to swim, tying themselves to the trunks to keep them afloat as they attempted to cross the vast river. Some still drowned. Others were shot when discovered by the Laotian border security patrols. A shiver went through Dad as he spotted the long length of vine trailing behind it, remembering that he was the only one in our family who knew how to swim.

"There's water in the boat," someone said in a hushed voice.

"Are we sinking?" my mother asked.

"Is there a hole in the boat?" the other woman asked, panic in her voice.

"No," said my father. "It's coming in over the sides. There are too many people in the boat; we're too heavy."

"Toss any extra belongings you have," one of the smugglers ordered. "Do it now or we'll all end up in the water!"

What little we had carried with us was quickly thrown overboard and left to drift down the river, but it wasn't enough, and Dad tried using one of his shoes to toss the water out. It was making too much noise, though, and one of the smugglers scolded him, so he resorted to scooping it out with his hands as quietly as he could.

Somehow the boat didn't sink, and we were all exhausted by the time the boat scraped shore on the other side. Anxious to get away from the river and any patrols that could come by at any moment, we all jumped out only to end up in quicksand. The two smugglers who had remained in the boat quickly pushed off, never to be seen again.

It took me a moment to realize what was happening when my feet slowly sunk into the ground. I tried lifting a leg and felt a suctioning around my foot, pulling it back into the sand. I was immediately reminded of the horror stories I'd heard about people getting stuck in quicksand.

Dad reached out for a nearby vine and managed to pull himself out before he sunk in too deep. He pulled me out first before assisting my older brother. Tobee thought this was all great fun, as he began to run across the sand so quickly he avoided being sucked back in.

"Tobee!" my father scolded as he struggled to pull Leh out. "Stand by your brother and be quiet!"

Meanwhile, Lucky and Mom were still stuck in the sand. As she looked to Mom, then to her own body sinking farther down, she was sure that she was going to die that night.

FREEDOM CROSSING

Suddenly she felt Dad's hand pull her out, and relief swept through her as she scrambled to safety where the rest of us kids were waiting. That feeling of relief didn't last long, though, as she glanced back and saw that the quicksand was now up to Mom's chest. And the look of sheer terror on our mother's face was something she had never seen before. Even Mom didn't see how she could get out of this. She continued to sink lower and lower into the quicksand while every moment with her family flashed before her eyes, along with everything she would never share with them again. She looked to Lucky, who was crying, overwhelmed by the thought of losing her mom. My mother thought to herself, at least my children are safe, even if I don't make it.

By this time, Thai guards had found us and were aiming their guns at our group.

"Leave her!" the guards shouted, not wanting to get caught by Laotian security any more than my parents.

Dad threw her the same vine he used to help us, but it didn't work; it was too short. Dad wasn't ready to give up on her. My father knew we hadn't made it this far, this close to freedom, only for him to lose the woman he loved. He looked around frantically, trying to find a branch or stick—anything to help her get out—to no avail.

FREEDOM CROSSING

My father had never been a religious man, but unsure of what he could do, he started praying. First he prayed to the spirits of his mother and father. Then he asked the Buddha to help. But nothing happened. He didn't know a lot about Christianity but had heard people talk about God. So he prayed to Him, making sure he covered every higher power he could think of.

"Please God," he begged. "If there is a God, please help me. I can't lose Khanthaly, I can't lose her!"

He looked around one last time, and there was a branch he hadn't noticed. It didn't seem very strong, but it was enough to give him hope, so he grabbed it anyway and frantically tossed it to my mother.

Lucky was watching from the shore, not daring to take her tear-filled eyes off of Mom. She watched Dad toss Mom the branch, thinking there's no way it's strong enough to get her out, not when she had sunk so deep.

But Mom reached for it, desperate for anything, and pushed it down beneath her feet as best she could. To her own amazement as well my Dad's and Lucky's, she was able to start walking up it until Dad could reach for her hand and help her the rest of the way. He immediately pulled her into his arms, a rare moment of public affection despite their conservative culture. Only moments ago he had been sure she wasn't going to make it, and now he was just thankful to be able to hold her again.

"We need to go," one of the guards called out. "It's not safe to remain on the shore."

"He's right," my father replied, releasing her to wipe the tears he hadn't even realized he'd been crying.

Together, we followed the guards away from the shore. We'd barely lost sight of the river when a boat motor was heard—a boat that carried Laos security guards, no doubt. My parents quickly looked at each other, their eyes wide. Had my mother still been stuck in the quicksand—had any of us still been on that shore—we would have been shot on sight, as the patrols had done countless times before. Lucky, Leh, Tobee, and I had no idea the significance of the passing boat we heard, but my parents knew how close we had come to being caught, how close we'd been to death.

Getting to Camp

As we neared the camp, escorted by the Thai security, all my mother could think about was that we were finally free. We'd escaped Laos and were all together. We were free.

But before we were actually allowed into the camp, we were taken to the attached detention center, where my parents were interrogated.

"What is your name?" a guard asked.

"Sisavath and Khanthaly," my mother told him, and he jotted it down.

"Last name?"

"We don't have a last name," Dad lied, not wanting anyone to be able to find out their occupation. They knew the main reason for this interrogation was to find out if they were spies from the Laotian government. Being government employees would surely suggest that they were, meaning they would be turned away. And once the Laotian government learned our family had tried to escape... my parents knew it would mean trouble for them.

The guard frowned. "Are you a criminal?"

"No," Mom said.

"Then why are you here?"

"Because we don't believe in communism," she told him. "We don't like the politics."

The guard scowled, continuing to make notes.

"Please," she begged. "We are poor. We don't have anything to eat and need your help."

He seemed satisfied by her answers. But that was only the first step to getting into camp.

"Once there's a room available for your family, you will be allowed into the camp."

"Oh, thank you," my mother said.

"How long will that be?" Dad asked.

"Who knows?" the guard shrugged. "There are a lot of people also waiting."

FREEDOM CROSSING

The guard led them to a large room where there must have been a hundred people already gathered.

"Until then," he told my parents, "you'll wait here."

My parents soon learned that the process of being given a room in the camp wasn't as simple as first come, first served, despite what they were told.

While the Thai guards may have looked down on the refugees, they still had their favorites and would sometimes give preferential treatment when assigning rooms to waiting families. Families who were being sponsored and preparing to leave the refugee camp were sometimes able to pass their living quarters along to someone by slipping a few bucks to the corrupt guards This meant that knowing someone already at camp could work to our advantage. So every night, my parents would go out and walk along the fence dividing the detainment center from the main camp area in the hopes of glimpsing a familiar face.

And they did. Through the chain link, my mother managed to spot a neighbor who happened to have escaped around the same time. After chatting for a while, the neighbor offered to sell their room to our family when they left.

FREEDOM CROSSING

We spent the next month waiting in the detainment center, eating the exact same rations day in and day out and sleeping on the floor with only a blanket between our weary bodies and the hard concrete.

But we were finally provided with a room in the Nong Khai refugee camp, a city in itself.

FREEDOM CROSSING

Lucky

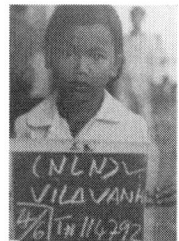
Leh

Tobee

Quito

At Nong Khai Camp. NLN: No Last Name

Life at Camp

The refugee camp occupied a large area in Nong Khai, Thailand. In the middle was a large field used for all kinds of sports and assemblies, while low bamboo bungalows lined the sides and end opposite the administrative building. Each bungalow was sectioned off into separate rooms, roughly 10ft x 8ft. One of these rooms housed our entire family. It was where we slept, cooked, and even bathed. There was no running water, and it soon became Lucky's job every morning to carry the pole with two buckets attached to collect our water ration for the day.

Every family was assigned a number (as seen in the camp picture), and that would be our ticket to collecting rations, including food. But by the time Thai guards pillaged it for themselves, there was barely enough to go around for the refugees. It could vary from day to day, but our allotment typically consisted of one egg, a handful of sticky rice, and one quarter of a chicken. That's what was supposed to feed our entire family each day. My mother became very creative with cooking what little we had, adding water to the egg to make it stretch further, and by the time we were done with that chicken piece, there wasn't a scrap left to it.

From the refugee camp, we would go on to a third country—a new permanent home. But the process could take months or even years. When the camp was finally shut down a few years later, the refugees remaining were sent back to Laos. While the Thai government had been pressed by the United Nations to provide the camp, Laotians were not welcomed in their country. Thai citizens feared that the Laotians would steal their jobs.

While at camp, my mother ran into yet another neighbor from Laos. Both women were looking for a way to better provide for their families while waiting for resettlement and came up with a plan for their own business.

Using another ounce of gold from the bracelet she had successfully carried across the Mekong, my mother would buy fabric for the neighbor to make sarongs out of. Together they sold the skirts in the thriving market set up in camp by the refugees, then split the profits. It wasn't long until they were making the equivalent of $20US each. Business was going so well that the neighbor soon decided she didn't need Mom's contribution now that she had enough money to buy her own fabric.

This time my father had a plan of his own. Using the last ounce of gold, he bought a samlor (Thai rickshaw) from another refugee who was leaving the camp for resettlement. Mom felt bad for him—an educated man who would now be paid to bike people to and fro. And my father was not a very strong man; he'd never done work this physical before. So before he took on fares, he practiced with our family, only crashing once while we were actually in it! But eventually he felt confident enough and he worked as much as he could, often from four in the morning until eight at night. It was hard and tiring, but he never gave it a second thought. If that was what it took to provide for his family, he did it without thinking twice. He'd even given up smoking and drinking since getting to camp, knowing that paying for such pleasures meant less for his family when they already had so little.

FREEDOM CROSSING

Even after a very long day, my father still made time for us every night. As we piled into the middle of the concrete floor, preparing for sleep, Dad would entertain us all with stories and jokes, and would teach us different fundamentals such as counting and left from right. Despite our living conditions, I still look back at those times with fondness. Six-year-old me couldn't imagine anything better than all of us being together.

Another evening ritual of ours was to walk around the camp, seeing as how there wasn't much in the way of entertainment in Nong Khai.

We were out one night when my dad heard someone calling his name. He was surprised when he turned to see one of his former students approaching him.

"Teacher!" she says. "When did you get here?"

"We arrived about two months ago," he answered.

"Not so long then. Do you know where you are going to yet?" she asked.

"It looks like we'll be going to France," my mother replied. "Sie has a niece there and he speaks French, so our odds are much better.

"France," the student said, "Wouldn't you rather go to the USA?"

"The USA," my dad said, looking at Mom. "We hadn't really given it any thought."

"America is much better," the student told us. "You can do anything there, so many more opportunities."

"But we don't know anyone there to help us out or sponsor us," Mom told her. "Doesn't that make it almost impossible?"

"Ah," she said. "But you know me. My boyfriend has a job working with American Embassy, doing the interviews. So if you'd really like to go to the US, I can help you."

"Really?" my father asked, his interest piqued. "You could do that?"

"Just put your application in, and he'll make sure it gets to the top. He and I have already been through the process," she explained. "But since we aren't married yet, it's been hard getting a sponsorship for the both of us."

"What do you think?" Dad asks Mom. "I know we were planning to go to France…"

"I'd rather go to the US," she says.

"Let's do it then. Let's put in our application."

My parents filled out the application, and in the box asking for our last name, they wrote in Keutla, my mother's maiden name. And from then on, we were the Keutla family.

FREEDOM CROSSING

Mom turned in the application, and sure enough, it was moved right to the top of the pile and my parents were scheduled for an interview the very next day.

With that done, all that was left was to wait for a sponsor. During that time, my parents attended classes provided by the United Nations where they learned basic phrases in English and how to use the currency.

Since we didn't know anyone already living in the US, our family was depending on the generosity of someone to support the emigration of our family into America. Being a family of six made it harder, but fate was on our side.

Across the world in Billings, Montana, Doctor Hagstrom and his wife Evie had recently been inspired by the humanitarian work of an acquaintance. With the help of their St. Luke's Episcopal Church, they managed to raise the $10,000 required to sponsor a family. And we were to be that family.

For two months my parents had been checking the board, waiting for our names to be posted. She knew that getting a family as large as ours sponsored was a gamble since many had been broken up, worried they may never leave the camp otherwise. But when she finally saw it, my mother started crying; she was so happy.

"Oh, Sie," she said as he put an arm around her. "It's our name, right? It's really happening."

"We're going to America," he replied, a huge grin on his face. "Where is Billings, Montana though?" he asked, noticing the location listed with our name.

Mom shrugged. "It's in the US. That's all that matters to me."

My father laughed, and she turned to some of the other people checking the board.

"Do you know where Montana is?" she asked.

"No," most of them replied.

"I've heard of it," someone finally chimed in. "They have Hmong people settled there, but I don't know if they have any Laotian there."

"Well then perhaps we'll be the first," Mom said, optimistic as ever about our future.

FREEDOM CROSSING

Leaving Asia

After only eight months at the camp, our family was leaving Nong Khai. Since my father no longer needed the samlor, he sold it to another refugee for $100, the same price he had paid for it. Certain that the hard part was over, Mom wanted thank the friend that had helped them escape by sending her all the money. But my father insisted that we keep $5 so that he could buy his children some treats when they arrived in America.

From camp, we boarded a bus and made the long ride into Bangkok to be processed along with the other refugees ready for resettlement.

After we were cleared by the "resettlement agency," we headed to the airport. At the airport, in a special waiting area, we were served a meal before our flight. We hadn't had so much food in a long time. We were overwhelmed by the luck we were having and how far we had made it on this journey.

When we boarded the plane, we were so excited. Of course, none of us kids had ever flown in a plane before. What was more exciting was that we were finally going to America! That excitement quickly become a feeling of nausea for Leh, though, as the motion of the plane taking off made her sick. Luckily, someone next to her recognized that she was about to throw up and reached for the barf bag in the seat pocket in front of her. "Here, use this."

After a layover in California, we arrived in Billings, Montana, where we were greeted by some of the members of St. Luke's Episcopal Church alongside our sponsor, Dr. Hagstrom and his wife.

Some of them were taking pictures, and they were all excited to see us. Some would comment and inquired, "How are you?", "Did you have a good flight?", or "So glad you are all finally here."

It was a bit overwhelming. Even though we couldn't understand anything they were saying, we felt very welcomed.

FREEDOM CROSSING

The Hagstroms then helped us get to our new home, an apartment they had rented for us in the central part of town not too far from the church.

When we entered, our eyes were immediately drawn to all the amenities: the refrigerator, stocked with fresh food, the electric stove, and the furniture, plus the TV. We were in awe. It all seemed so luxurious compared to what we were used to back in Laos and our living situation in Thailand. The apartment had three bedrooms and a bathroom. The rooms had beds, and the bathroom was even supplied with all kinds of toiletries like shampoo, soap, and towels.

Mom and Dad claimed the bedroom with the full size bed. Mother sat down on the plushy bed, and with a smile spreading across her face, she bounced up and down on it, unable to contain her excitement. She looked up at Dad, who was standing a few feet from the bed.

"We did it, Sie. We're here. We're free!"

He walked over and sat down next to her, a grin on his face to match her own. "Yes we did."

Adjusting

The church generously supported our family for six months with rent, food, and clothes. During that time, they also helped my parents find ways to make it on their own.

My parents had learned a little English back at the camp, but not enough to get a job, so the first thing Dad did was go to school. He would ride his bicycle to school every day. After only three months, he felt ready and asked our sponsor to help him find a job.

He put in applications for housekeeping at a local hotel and for a cook at St. Vincent's Hospital.

Between the two, he was hoping to get the cook position, thinking that he would be able to bring the leftovers home to the family.

As luck would have it, he did get offered a job in the hospital kitchen…as a dishwasher making $3.25 an hour, which was the minimum wage at the time. It wasn't exactly the job he was hoping for, but it was better than nothing. He also knew it was just a starting point. He was assured that there would be an opportunity to work his way up with experience and training.

After working a couple of months, they started training him as a cook's helper while still keeping him on pots and pans. During his training period, he learned everything they needed him to do. He learned to keep inventory of supplies, how to set the buffet including salad bar, and the preparation and cooking of each menu item. After four months he was finally promoted to cook's helper. But much to his disappointment, he didn't get to take the leftovers home. Turned out that was against their policy.

He did, however, get to eat free meals during his shift. Those leftovers, which he always tried to save, were allowed to be brought home.

While working, he still continued with evening school, finishing class at 10 p.m. and then heading to work for an 11 p.m. shift. The bike was still his only source of transportation to and from where he needed to be. Winter in Montana can be brutal, with inches (and sometimes feet) of snow and below-zero temperatures. Not the best condition for cyclists.

With not much of an option at the time, Dad kept relying on his bike. The snow would stick to the wheels, requiring him to clean it off every block before continuing.

This motivated him to save up enough money to buy his first car—a Toyota Celica for $225. The thing was a clunker, stalling almost every time he stopped at a red light. At least it was warmer than the bicycle, and he was proud to be a car owner.

The first few months were considerably harder for Mom.

From the moment she had decided they should leave Laos, she had only been thinking about all the horrible things they would be leaving behind and all the wonderful opportunities waiting for them in a country not ruled by a communist government. She hadn't considered what life would be like for her personally in America.

Soon after our arrival, Mom found out she was pregnant—something she hadn't been expecting.

FREEDOM CROSSING

Less than a year after we settled into Montana, my youngest brother, Luke, was born, named after the church that made our life in America possible. Coincidently, he was born on my birthday. Whenever I got annoyed with him as kids, he always liked to remind me that he was my birthday present.

But beyond Dad and all us kids, Mom had no family and no friends. She didn't speak English, and being the only Laotian family in Billings, there was no one for her to even talk to. She didn't know how to drive and was stuck at home.

It was a drastic change from living in Vientiane with all of her brothers and sisters nearby. She'd also had her job at an office and friends there. Without her extended family, friends, and a meaningful job to go to, she was feeling lonely. It also made it harder that she was craving authentic Laotian food and couldn't find any of the necessary ingredients in the local grocery stores.

Eventually Mom befriended another Laotian woman in our complex whose husband was Hmong. Mom soon came to depend on Bagien for getting around and answering questions about the new culture.

"Why don't you get your own car?" Bagien would often ask.

"What difference would that make? I don't have my license," Mom responded.

"Then get one.

"It's too hard," Mom sighed, frustrated that life in America had not turned out as she had originally hoped.

"Look at the Hmong people," Bagien shot back. "They lived in the mountains of Laos and had no need to drive a car. But it is different here and now most of them have learned to drive."

"Well, I don't want to learn to drive a car." Mom crossed her arms in defiance. "I don't want to go to school, I don't want to study, I don't want to do anything!"

"What about that old lady from the mountain? If she can do it with little education, so can you, Khanthaly," Bagien said, not giving up so easily.

After rethinking what her friend had said, Mom decided to take on the challenge of bettering her spoken English as well as her reading and writing skills. She enrolled in adult ESL classes. Not feeling completely confident, she also decided to go to driving school. She found it difficult and struggled in class, but she kept persevering. It took her several attempts—three times to be exact—for her to pass the test to get her driver's license. She kept remembering what Bagien had said about the

FREEDOM CROSSING

Hmong lady. That pushed Mom not to give up. She knew she could do it too.

While we were in Thailand, we had heard that it snowed a lot in Montana. So when we arrived in the middle of June, we expected to find snow. Clearly, we had no concept of the summer or winter months. With Laos being so close to the equator, we'd never experienced a real changing of seasons. Leh wanted to see snow, so every day she would wake up to look out the window, hoping for the cold white stuff to fall from the sky, only to be disappointed.

We kept asking one of our sponsors about it, so they explained to us when winter was. Since we were so curious about snow, they decided to take our family to Bear Tooth Pass, up in the mountains. As we were riding in the van, getting closer to the top,- we could see spots of what looked like white paint along the roadside and on top of the surrounding mountains. It was SNOW!

The van pulled over, and we were encouraged to go play in it. The second I stepped in, my feet sank, and I was immediately startled, remembering the quicksand. But I soon learned we weren't in any danger and was able to enjoy playing in it.

FREEDOM CROSSING

Shortly after our arrival was the start of school. And since none of us kids spoke much English, most of that first year was spent in ESL. Leh, who normally would have been in fourth grade, started in the second grade. It was a challenge in the beginning for her, not being able to communicate. Everyone at school understood it was her second language, though, and rather than make fun of her, they would try to help by correcting things. She picked it up pretty quickly and was soon conversing more confidently with people. In the end, she loved the English language and was excited to learn it.

Being seven, they started me in Kindergarten, and I remember sitting in class and having no clue what they were talking about. But the teachers were really nice, and like the rest of my siblings, I was eventually able to speak English with ease.

That first autumn also brought the holiday season, an altogether new experience for us as we didn't really celebrate holidays in Laos other than the New Year.

Halloween was the first holiday we experienced, and we kids loved the idea of dressing up along with everyone else. We couldn't really afford costumes, though, so we just made our own with whatever we could find. Leh went through

FREEDOM CROSSING

Mom's closet and found a dress that she could pretend to be a princess in. She loved putting outfits together in general, and despite most of our clothes being second-hand, she would often get compliments on her ensembles.

Then Christmas came.

Our family came home one day to find one of our sponsors waiting for us with a small tree and all the trimmings.

As they helped us set up the tree, they taught us about Christmas, what it meant, and the traditions. It was all very exciting for our family, especially for us kids.

Wrapped packages were placed beneath the tree, and we were told we couldn't open them until Christmas Day. But we couldn't help ourselves. We would peek inside and shake the presents trying to determine what they could be. We wondered what other holidays there were and if we would get gifts then as well.

Khanthaly's Egg Rolls

Opportunity struck for my struggling mother when a friend of our family moved to Seattle. The mother had been delivering newspapers and asked Mom if she would like to take it over. Mom was reluctant since she still didn't speak much English, but the woman showed her what to do, and Mom took it on.

Oftentimes my father would help her since he didn't have class in the morning. On their way home from delivering the papers, they would pick up empty cans they found along the way. We would all help in crushing the cans to be cashed in at the recycling facility. With the extra money, Dad would buy a six-pack of Sunkist from the nearby convenience store for us to enjoy as we hung out together on the front steps of the apartment. My parents were embarrassed by the whole situation of having to pick up cans for spare money, but my siblings and I never noticed they were bothered about it. We were happy to get to drink soda and be together. Those were fond memories for us.

The people at St. Luke's were always trying to find ways to help our parents earn extra money, as they understood how it would benefit us.

One day, one of the sponsors approached my mother.

"Khanthaly, I was wondering if you could help me?" she asked.

"Okay?"

"I'm hosting an event and was hoping you could clean my house for me. I'll pay you."

"Sure, I can help you," my mother told her.

When Mom was done, the woman was impressed.

"Would you be interested in doing this again?" she asked. "To make more money?"

"Maybe," Mom answered.

"Because I have a friend who is looking to hire a housekeeper."

"Oh, I don't know," my mother said, worried about letting someone down. "I'm not sure I would know how to do it."

"Don't worry," the woman said. "She'll show you how to do it."

"Well, I suppose," Mom finally agreed.

So the sponsor took Mom to the friend's house and showed her what to do. The new client loved it so much that she told *her* friends and neighbors what a good job Mom did.

It wasn't long before the referrals kept coming. Suddenly the housecleaning business she never intended to start was booming—so much, in fact, that she decided to quit the newspaper business. Lucky usually took care of us while Mom and Dad worked, but Mom sometimes had to bring us younger kids with her, especially Luke.

Despite business going so well, Mom still struggled with her position. Compared to the work she was doing back in Laos, cleaning other people's toilets was a dirty job—a low job. It was hard work that she wouldn't have been doing if it weren't for her children. And when no one was looking, she would often break down in tears. But then she would think about Khuanmany and stop crying, knowing that one day she was going to bring her daughter to the USA. She was going to keep working until she had enough money to bring her home.

While my mother was doing the housecleaning, she decided to participate in the job training offered through the refugee office. Not completely content with cleaning other people's homes, she wanted to be a cook.

She had already been making egg rolls and bringing them to church for potlucks or giving them to clients as gifts. I can still remember riding around with her as she delivered the warm egg rolls to everyone. Their mouth-watering aroma would fill the whole car, making me crave one for myself.

Eventually people started asking for them, and she would sell them, usually charging no more than enough to cover the cost of making them, if even that.

So the refugee office connected her with Happy Garden, a Chinese restaurant in Billings. She would work eight hours a day, six days a week with a half-hour break. The owner there kept her as busy as possible. Every day he would put a list of things for her to do on the board. When she finished the list, he would just put more jobs on it. For three months this continued, with the owner not actually teaching her anything. But as she watched, she couldn't help thinking that she could do better.

FREEDOM CROSSING

One day we went to the summer fair held at a nearby park. Mom noticed the food vendors there. She saw a lot of people waiting in line for tacos and waffle cookies but didn't see any Asian food stands. She thought this would be a perfect place to start selling her egg rolls to the public. Walking around the various booths, she asked how they were able to sell there and was given the name of the person responsible for procuring the food vendors.

It wasn't long before she was tracking down Stacy.

"Excuse me," Mom said, approaching her. "I would like to sell my egg rolls here. How would I do that?"

"You need a business license and insurance," Stacy told her. "And a kitchen for the prep work."

"A license and insurance," Mom murmured.

"It's very hard to get the license," Stacy warned her. "You need to go through the health department."

"Thank you," Mom said, nodding. "I will look into it."

When she was done with the job training, Mom went back to housecleaning but started working on a plan to be selling at the fair by the next summer.

FREEDOM CROSSING

We had since moved to a home of our own on Broadwater, and she turned our garage into her "kitchen." When it was ready, she called the Health Department to come inspect it.

"So," the inspector said as he was checking things off on his clipboard, "what should I put down as your business name?"

"My business name?" Mom hadn't thought that far ahead yet. Then she started thinking of how everyone would ask for Khanthaly's egg rolls.

"Khanthaly's Egg Rolls," she told the health inspector.

And just as she had planned, Mom was selling egg rolls at the summer fair the next year. And they were a hit! Everyone kept asking where they could buy her egg rolls beyond the fair, but she had to tell them that they couldn't.

Later she spotted another Asian family selling their egg rolls at the Farmer's Market. And sure enough, Mom applied for an additional license that allowed her to sell at the market.

Still, people kept asking where else they could get the egg rolls. Did she have a restaurant?

Mom decided it was time to buy a trailer and start her own food truck. She tried going to the bank and asking for a loan but was declined. Not to be deterred, Dad agreed to let her sell his car so they could get the trailer. When the trailer was built,

FREEDOM CROSSING

Mom found an ideal downtown location for it at the TransWestern Plaza. The best part was that it was free to park there! You can still find my mother there most days selling to the lunch crowd.

The trailer did very well there during the warm months when people would venture outside for lunch. Her customers kept asking for more.

Then one day, the perfect spot became available next to the IGA off of Grand Avenue. Everything she needed was already there; she just had to sign the lease.

In 1994, my mother's dream came true when Khanthaly's Egg Rolls officially opened as a restaurant.

Almost since the beginning, my parents had been sending money whenever they could to our Uncle, who was still caring for Khuanmany, and writing to her when she was old enough to correspond.

When Khuanmany was fourteen, my mother went back to Laos for the first time since leaving. Mom explained to her why they fled and why they left her behind, telling Khuanmany that she could come to America with them once she finished high school there in Laos.

In 1995 my parents were finally able to bring Khuanmany home. Khuanmany was excited to be reunited with siblings she didn't even remember but was disappointed when she found that most of us had left home by that time, either away at college or already starting families of our own.

And even though she had finished high school back in her village, she was required to complete a couple years of high school in the US before going on to college.

Adjusting to American life was probably the hardest for her, but in the end she was glad that she made the decision to come live with her parents. She has been able to help out the family that she grew up with back in Laos and knows they are better off because of the support she has given them.

FREEDOM CROSSING

No Place Like Billings

While most of us kids, myself included, have moved away from Billings, my parents still live there and wouldn't have it any other way.

When our family first arrived, we practically doubled the Laotian population of Billings. Most refugees headed to Montana ended up in Missoula. Our parents thought about moving elsewhere, often visiting other states and bigger cities, thinking life might be better. Most of the larger areas offered a Laotian community with stores, businesses, and customs that were familiar to my parents. But then they began to worry that moving to a big city might not be in our best interest. They'd heard too many stories about kids joining gangs or deciding not to go to school. So in the end, they decided to stay right where they were and have never regretted it.

Over time, a few more Laotian refugees were brought to Billings, but after a year, most of them would move away. There weren't many jobs for them—usually cleaning or working at a hotel. And most of the kids didn't like living in such a small city; it wasn't exciting enough for them.

But my parents stayed here for us. And I think we all agree it was the right decision.

If we had been part of a larger Laotian community, my parents wouldn't have struggled as much, which means they wouldn't have pushed themselves as much. They exhibited a work ethic that has been ingrained in all of us children, and we are forever grateful for it.

Gratitude

<u>Lucky</u>

I remember Dad coming home with burns, and Mom's knees always hurting because she'd spent all day having to kneel down and scrub floors. They worked so hard just to put food on the table. Eventually they were able to start their own business and next thing I knew, we had food, *good* food, and candy and all this stuff. They came pretty far; they did great.

<u>Leh</u>

I don't recall much about the day we arrived, but I do remember thinking how nice all these people from the church were. I felt lucky, we were so lucky that these people were taking care of us.

Growing up in Montana, there wasn't a lot of diversity as far as different cultures. We stuck out like a sore thumb. We were one of only two Asian families, yet I never felt like I was discriminated against at all. People were very accepting of our family. They were so benevolent and so kind. It amazes me how supportive the community was. I'm so happy and so glad that we're here. Everything that we were taught and given really helped shape who we are today. We're really fortunate for that. I think about it all the time. And especially how Mom and Dad gave up so much so that we could have this. I think they're pretty happy with how we all turned out.

Tobee

I want to thank Mom and Dad for giving me life and for teaching me how to love and that if you work hard you can achieve anything in life. Most of all, the biggest thanks is for when they made the ultimate sacrifice to come to America 37 years ago to give me and my siblings the good life that America had to offer us. Finally, I want to thank St. Luke's Church for sponsoring us and for teaching us the English language, the American culture, and to believe in God.

Quito
I'm really proud of my parents. Having to let go of what life was like in Laos to come to a place, not knowing anything about it, with five kids… They did great.

Khuanmany
Despite how hard it was when I first arrived in the US, I'm glad I came.

Back in Laos, the kids are growing up, they've not only graduated high school, they've gone to college. They've built a new house and their life is better. It makes me feel good because I have a duty to them. I still help them out, still support them. If I can do that for them, then I am glad I am here.

When I first came here, it was different, hard even, and it felt like it took me forever to get used to it. But it made me a better, stronger person. It's how you learn.

Luke
Growing up they were strict, they were working hard to provide for the family. I thought of them as being too tough, but maybe that's how it is

for all kids. Now that they've retired and with me being home consistently, I think my relationship with them is great. I talk to them about anything.

It was a pain in the butt working for them, but now I'd rather exhaust myself than see them work.

I'm closer with the older siblings now than when I was growing up. It's nice to hang out with my family and talk to them.

Through their determination to get to America and fighting the odds, coming in and not even having a plan, and working hard, their number one goal was not for them to have a better life, but for their children to have a better life, I think they've reached that goal. They've worked hard; their children are grown and taken care of.

I know that they can rest easy knowing that they've accomplished what they set out to do.

When I get frustrated, I think about my parents coming to America with five dollars and five kids, and they made it happen. And they did that because they wanted us to do whatever we wanted to do. And that's what I'm doing. I'll never forget that.

FREEDOM CROSSING

Acknowledgements

I want to take this moment to thank all of my siblings—Lucky, Leh, Tobee, Khuanmany, and Luke—for collaborating with me to make this happen, taking the time to talk on the phone and pulling back memories that span back as far as 30 years ago. This truly is our story; your words and thoughts were so vital in putting this together for our parents. I cannot express how much your love and encouragement went into making this happen.

I also want to thank Jolene Irons, who has been so indispensable with her experience in writing, her insights, and for keeping me on track.

To all the families at St. Luke's Church, the Hagstroms, Harts, Leeds, MacKays, Stroskys, Searls, and I'm sure many more whom I've forgotten, who dedicated their time and resources to supporting a Laotian family.

FREEDOM CROSSING

Quito Keutla is a Transformational Success Coach, speaker, author, and real estate entrepreneur. He lives in Renton, Washington with his wife and three children.

Made in the USA
Columbia, SC
05 June 2019